A n00b's Guide to Using Autodesk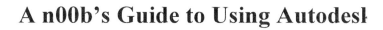

By Gregory Marlow

Tech N00b Books

www.techn00b.com

Table of Contents

Introduction

Technology bombards us with new inventions and innovations almost daily. But when presented with a new gizmo or gadget, an artist's first thought (even if not spoken aloud) is usually: "Yeah that's nice...but can I make art with it?" The personal computer was co-opted almost immediately by wily artists painting one pixel at a time or even drawing with text in the form of ASCII art. The computer has advanced quickly as a tool that artists use to express and create. In fact, many modern illustrators and comic artists work almost exclusively in digital form.

So it is no surprise that the advent of the smartphone and the tablet quickly developed the capabilities to create on the go. Many software packages have thrown their hat into this arena, but one has managed to bridge the gap between the different platforms almost seamlessly; Autodesk SketchBook.

In this book we will explore the PC/Mac, Tablet, and Mobile versions of Autodesk SketchBook. We will talk about what is similar and what is different about each platform and how it can serve artists in the office, at home, or on the move. But most importantly we will talk about how artists can use it to create art.

Autodesk SketchBook...Which one?

Let's imagine you walked into your local hardware store and found an employee willing to help you. He asks how he can help, and you tell him you are needing a tool.

"What kind of tool?" he asks.

"A really shiny one," you reply.

This is how many people shop for software. With all the 2D art creation software on the market it wouldn't take very long to spend your annual salary on a bunch of packages you don't need or will never use. So it is important to go into these decisions well informed.

Autodesk SketchBook comes in four major flavors:

SketchBook Pro

This is the full-featured version available for the PC and Mac. SketchBook Pro has every feature that is available in the SketchBook repertoire.

At roughly fifty dollars, it comes in at a much lower price tag than a lot of other 2D asset creation tools. But that is because it knows its place in the market. SketchBook was designed for the task of getting ideas out of your head and onto the computer, quickly and efficiently. It is exactly what the name says. It is a digital sketching option. And because it is not trying to be everything to everyone, it is extremely efficient and user-friendly.

Don't confuse this with the idea that SketchBook is weak or featureless. Many artists use SketchBook as their primary workhorse to create concepts, designs, and even finalized polished illustrations. It provides a rich tool set for artists to achieve a great range of rendering techniques without being bloated and difficult to use.

The one thing it is lacking, however, is the ability to put it in your back pocket and take it anywhere you want to go.

SketchBook Mobile

Okay, so you probably don't really want to put your iPhone or Android in your back pocket; you might break it. But smartphones have revolutionized the way we work while on the go. SketchBook Mobile allows users to quickly capture their ideas on their iPhone, iPod touch, or Android powered device.

Most mobile devices lack pressure sensitivity, making the input options a bit more limited. But SketchBook has a few creative workarounds that make this less of an issue. When using your finger as an input device, accuracy becomes more difficult to control. These are problems that all mobile devices face at this time. Most people would not decide to illustrate their magnum opus on their iPhone, but it is more than capable for sketching a rough landscape while sitting on a park bench or getting a quick concept down when you don't have a pen, paper, or Wacom Cintiq handy. And at about two dollars, it is an app that is definitely worth having.

SketchBook Pro for iPad and Android

The tablet market has exploded over the last few years. SketchBook Pro for iPad and Android is a bit like a bridge between the mobile and the full featured PC and Mac version. Tablets provide a bit more screen real estate over the smaller mobile devices and also allow you a bit more leeway on accuracy. For the most part, they are not pressure sensitive but still offer many creative options. Once you accept the tool for what it is, you will see that it is actually a pretty impressive app for only five dollars.

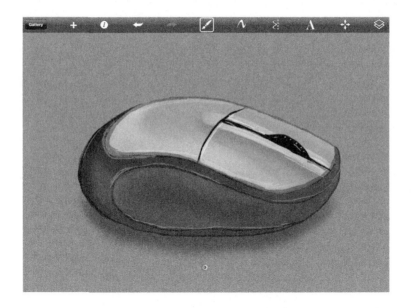

SketchBook Express and Mobile Express

Are you cheap, poor, or just can't figure out how to get your credit card associated with the app store? Well then you are in luck, because you can still use a version of SketchBook on your phone or tablet for free. The Express and Mobile Express versions differ only slightly, but both offer more simplified tool sets and options than the full version of the app while still giving you a lot of the same sketching features. In the end, it does its job well by getting you addicted to the software. The more you play with the free Express version the cheaper $1.99 and $4.99 start to look in the app store.

Keeping all this straight is difficult, so to help you with your decision making, here is a quick breakdown of the differences between the different versions of the software. But with the reasonable pricing, no one would blame you for owning them all.

Input Devices

A program, no matter how advanced, intuitive, or expensive, is useless unless you have a good way to interact with it. Digital art creators have struggled with this since the first artist sat down in front of a computer and stared doubtfully at the keyboard. Many creative solutions have come along since then, and artists now have many ways to input their creativity into SketchBook.

SketchBook Pro for PC and Mac

The Mouse and Keyboard

Yeah, I know what you are thinking; we have all struggled to write our name with the spray can in MS Paint. The problem with the mouse as an input device is also its biggest perk. A mouse does not lend itself well to gestural, sketchy line making. But it is very good device to use in times when high exact precision is required. SketchBook has several options for creators of technical art, and sometimes those elements will be most easily controlled using the mouse.

The keyboard has played a large role in much of the 2D art packages in the past. Tool selection, options, and brush adjustments are often delegated to a keyboard shortcut to allow for a quick, customizable work flow. Although there is nothing wrong with this and many artists work happily that way, SketchBook addresses these selection and manipulation tools with a creative user interface. It allows the user to make these kinds of adjustments on the screen without having to dig around and find the keyboard. Although shortcut keys do exist for many of the tools in SketchBook, it is the lack of their necessity that makes it so intuitive to use. Technology shy artists can pick up SketchBook and start using it with only a few, quick instructions.

Graphics Tablet and Displays

Remember the first time you ever used a crayon? Probably not, because most likely you were about two or three years old. Most people have been using writing implements for almost as long as they have been walking. So a pen or stylus is a natural choice for an input device and an artist's dream come true.

A company called Wacom has cornered most of the market on digital drawing tablets and displays. They offer several options and lines of graphics tablets ranging in sizes and pressure sensitivities. Many are very affordable for the everyday consumer starting at around $75. It takes a little while to get used to drawing on one surface while looking at another, but once you do, your work flow will drastically improve. However, less popular and even more affordable versions are available on online auction sites as well.

Wacom also offers an interactive display line called the Cintiq. These options are much more expensive starting at around $900 for the 12 inch model. Although expensive, they have the added benefit of being able to see the lines you create appear under the tip of your pen.

Graphics tablets and displays are perfect for using SketchBook Pro because of the intuitive GUI. It allows the user to work in a much more traditional manner when creating art.

Tablet PCs and Slates

This option could be called "the poor man's Cintiq." Many companies have developed laptops with interactive touch screens for quick input. Although many of the needs these machines were created for have been taken over by iPads and Android tablets, they still have the upper hand in a few areas over tablets and portable devices. First, most of these tablet PC's and Slates are running full versions of Windows and OSx, meaning you can install the full featured version of SketchBook Pro. Also, unlike most tablets, many tablet PC's and Slates come with pressure sensitive screens. This means a world of difference to an artist because the pressure sensitivity can control many of your line attributes including thickness, opacity, and texture. Having this added dimension of input gives the artist more control over the work they create.

However, many companies have abandoned the tablet PC's and Slates in order to cash in on the booming tablet market. Although several companies do still create new Slates and tablet computers, many of the older ones can be found used for quite cheap. In fact, many of the illustrations in this book were created on a tablet PC that was purchased used for $200.

When shopping for a tablet computer or slate, look for one that has an "Active Digitizer" display. This will give you the pressure sensitive options similar (although not quite as detailed) as the Wacom options.

Tablets and Mobile Devices

Finger

Tablets have caused us all to regress to our finger-painting youth. But despite the seemingly primitive drawing option, your fingers do a pretty similar job as a pen, except you have ten of them (hopefully). The tablet and SketchBook's interface utilizes your multi-digitedness in several creative ways, including a pinch zoom and pan and the ability to bring up the menus by simply touching three fingers to the screen at once.

Fingers come with one drawback though; they are wide. This means you have much less control on the precision of your lines when you are using your finger to draw. If you are drawing a line that is one tenth the width of your finger, it is hard to determine what part of your finger will be sensed by the screen first to create the line.

Capacitive Stylus

This issue with precision when using your finger lies in the tablet itself. The Apple and Android devices utilize a capacitive screen to sense touch. This means that the screen sensor is looking for an electrically conductive object to touch the screen. A stick is not conductive, nor is a pencil or an ink pen, and it is highly recommended that you do not try to use these items as a drawing implement on your tablet or mobile device. However, the human body is conductive, so when your finger touches the screen it recognizes it. That is why your Nintendo DS stylus doesn't work on your iPhone.

However, many companies have addressed this need for a stylus that is conducive for tablets and mobile devices. You can find them for very affordable prices online. They are not quite as precise as a Wacom stylus. Due to the capacitive nature of the device it is more like drawing with a pencil eraser than a pencil lead, but it is significantly more precise than a finger and may provide the extra detail you need.

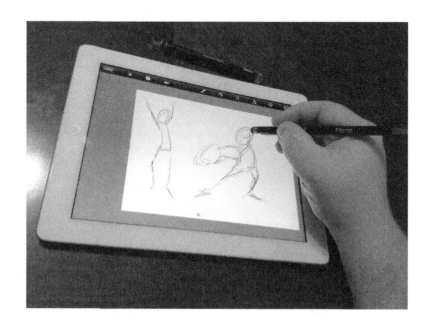

Using SketchBook

SketchBook utilizes several user interface elements to help make the program simple and easy to use and still maintain a very small learning curve. With just a few quick instructions and a few minutes of practice any traditional artist can use SketchBook without feeling overburdened by the program itself. And although not all of the different versions of SketchBook work exactly the same, many of the same user interface elements persist across the different devices. The difficulty many programs have with adapting for the tablets and mobile devices are non-existent for SketchBook because of its touch friendly design in the first place.

Let's explore the program on the computer first because it is the version that offers the largest amount of features. Then we will move on to the other versions for comparison.

PC and Mac

When you first open SketchBook Pro on the PC or Mac, it will seem a little sparse and simple. But if you expand out all of the different UI elements you will have something that resembles the image below. Let's explore each of these UI elements.

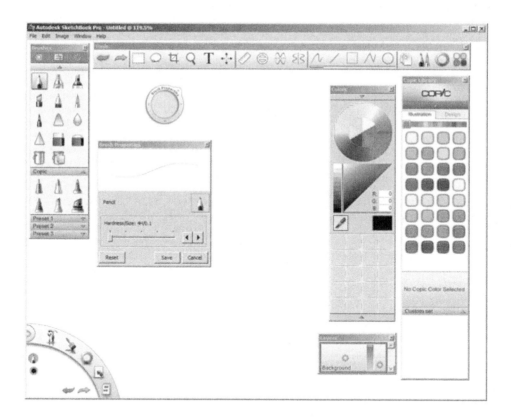

The large white field in the background is your canvas. This is where you will be making all your marks and creating your sketches. It also serves as a bit of a backdrop for all your tool bars.

Lagoon

In the bottom left-hand corner of the screen is a quarter of a circle with icons on it. This is called the Lagoon. It is a quick palette of tools and options that takes up very little space. It allows you to quickly access some of the most used tools and functions without having to clutter up the screen with unnecessary UI elements.

Inside the Lagoon is your currently selected tool as well as that tool's brush size. The red and green arrows are the undo and redo buttons respectively.

Along the perimeter of the lagoon are icons. If you click on one of these icons, a circle of additional icons will pop up around your mouse. This is called a *Marking Menu.* You will find marking menus throughout SketchBook, and it is one of the things that make SketchBook quick and easy to use with a single input device. This simple UI style allows a large range of buttons to be at your fingertips, while still keeping the interface clean and simple.

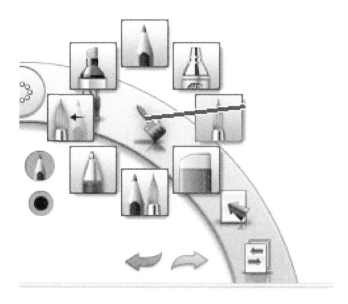

Going clockwise around the lagoon, the first button is your interface controls. The second button with the image of a hammer and wrench accesses view controls, canvas transform tools, rulers, layers, and symmetry. The brush button brings up your brushes and palettes options. The color wheel button brings up a marking menu containing some simple swatches and an option to access the color editor. The next button, depicted as a piece of paper with an arrow, contains your selection, editing, and layer transform tools. And the last button has basic program operations, such as open, save, and new.

Along the top of the interface is a traditional menu with five options: File, Edit, Image, Window, and Help. Under the Window menu option check all six menu items. This will open all the different major UI Windows.

Tools Panel

The Tools Panel is the long thin bar of icons pictured below.

Many of the functions found on this tool bar are also found in the menu and lagoon. The first two buttons are for undo and redo. The second set of icons cover selection, text, and navigation of the canvas. The third set of tools on the tool bar are for symmetry and rulers, which allow you to draw at specific angles or arcs.

The next section of five icons allows you to choose what sort of lines and shapes you want to make. The first squiggly line allows you to freely make marks on the paper. The second straight line only allows you to draw perfectly straight lines. The square creates perfectly square and rectangular shapes, and the circle makes circles and ellipses. The zig zaggy line is the polyline tool. It works similarly to the line tool except that it allows you to make multiple successive lines all connected. This allows you to draw out rigid polygonal shapes quickly.

The last four icons in the toolbar turn on and off UI Elements. You will notice that these buttons do the same thing as checking and un-checking the last four options under the Windows menu item.

The redundancy between the Tools Panel, Menu, and the lagoon is a good example of how SketchBook gives different users multiple options to do the same actions. This allows the user to choose the way they want to work. Some people like icons, some like shortcut keys, some like marking menus, and some like the lagoon.

Brushes

The brushes panel is where you can choose pre-made brushes, create custom brushes, or edit existing brushes. Some artists use the brush panel a great deal to alter and create brushes for a variety of effects, textures, and styles. Other artists simply pick a few basic brushes and stick to those religiously. But whatever your preferences, you can easily find or create a brush that will let you make the kind of marks you need to create your sketches and illustrations.

At the top of the brushes panel you will find three icons. The first icon opens a small UI element that allows you to quickly alter your brush size. Simply click in the center and drag from side to side. This brush resizer shows up in the tablet and mobile versions of SketchBook as well, with one key difference. The mobile and tablet versions allow you to resize the brush but also to change the opacity of the brush by dragging up and down.

The second icon at the top of the brushes panel opens the brush properties. This window can range in size and content. This panel is where you can alter settings for each of the current brushes. Since the PC and Mac versions of SketchBook recognize pressure sensitivity you can alter the way pen pressure effects the size and opacity of the brush. You can also alter texture and shape options to create unique styles of custom brushes.

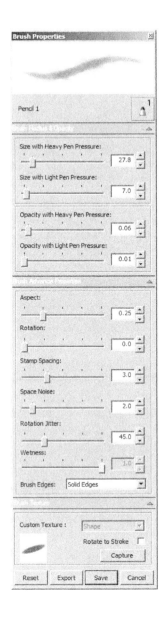

The third icon at the top of the brushes panel activates a marking menu. This marking menu gives you options to create new brushes and brush sets. When you create a new brush, you are given the option to start with a base brush and then you can alter that brush by editing the brush properties till you have a custom brush that fits your need.

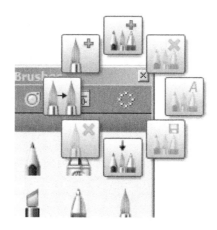

Below the three icons on the brushes menu are your brushes and brush sets. The top fourteen brushes are the base set. Each brush makes marks on the canvas differently, each mimicking its real world equivalent. For example, if you make a dark green mark with the marker brush, you cannot create a lighter mark on top of that mark, only darker. When first opening SketchBook, it is a good idea to spend some time experimenting with these brushes to learn how they work.

Below the base brushes are different brush sets. SketchBook comes with several presets of brushes for you to explore and use. You can also create your own sets for brushes you know you will use often. If you do a lot of comic art then you can create a set of brushes for inking and cross-hatching. If you work in a more painterly style, you can create a set of brushes that mimic the way you would work on a real world painting. Whatever your preferences, you can quickly make a set of brushes that help you create the way you want.

Color Editor

The Color Editor is where you will be choosing and creating the colors you wish to use in your sketches, drawings, and paintings. If you have used any other graphics programs in the past, it works very similarly.

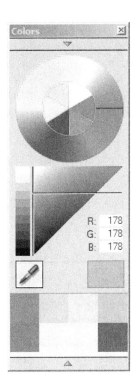

At the top, you have a color wheel which will allow you to select the hue. At the center of the color wheel are the primary and secondary colors for a quick access.

Below the color wheel is a triangular shape known as the *Slider* that allows you to select and change the saturation, lightness, and darkness of the previously selected hue. For example, if you need a dark blue color, simply select the color of blue you want on the wheel then click in the triangle to choose the correct saturation and shade. Side to side changes the saturation and up and down changes the lightness and darkness. Along the left side of the triangle is a row of gray-scale swatches for quick selection.

Directly below the gray scale swatches is an eyedropper which you can use to sample colors from your image. Holding down the Alt key will allow you to quickly access the eyedropper tool.

The *Swatch*, or current color, is displayed in a rectangle to the right of the eye dropper tool, beneath a listing of the RGB values. Of course these values can be changed manually if you know the exact value you need.

Below the eyedropper and swatch are rows of empty squares. This is your custom color palette. Once you have the color that you want, you can click and drag the swatch to one of the color palette squares to save that color for future use.

The Mac version of the Color Editor is a bit more elaborate. Along the top of the color editor are five alternative color mixing methods. Each is simply a different way of choosing from the same range of colors. The option you choose is all a matter of personal preference.

Copic

If you have SketchBook pro 2011, and you have updated to the free service packs two or three, then you have an additional option for choosing colors. The new menu is called the Copic Library. Copic is a Japanese marker company that creates a series of 358 different marker colors that can be mixed to create additional colors. If you are a fan of those markers, the new copic library allows you to choose from the various available marker colors and their mixed variations.

Also, in the brush menu you will notice a Copic brush set containing four Copic markers, one Copic drawing pen, and one Copic multi-liner. The combined brushes and library allows artists who are fans of Copic markers to make a quick and cheap transition to digital and still retain their work methods and styles.

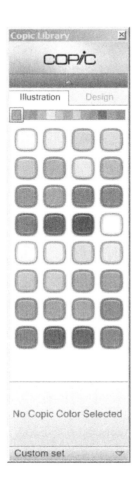

Layer Editor

Layers are a great way to organize the elements that make up your image. A real world comparison is to imagine each layer is a transparent piece of plastic on which you can draw and paint. If you lay each piece of plastic on top of each other, the combined images make up one composite image.

Layers work the same way in SketchBook. They are organized with the top most layer in the layer editor being the top visible layer in the image.

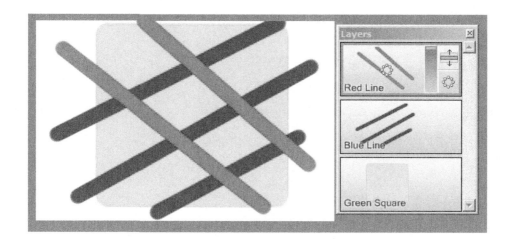

In this way, layers in SketchBook work similarly to layers in other 2D applications. However, SketchBook takes a very user-friendly and gestural approach to layers. Clicking on the dotted circle above the layer name brings up a marking menu with options to create, delete, duplicate, hide, lock, merge, and rename the selected layer. This marking menu condenses time consuming tasks to simple flicks of the pen.

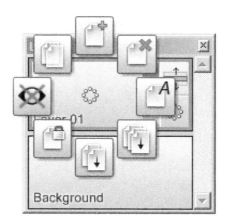

Along the right side of the selected layer you will see a vertical slider and two buttons. The slider allows you to quickly change the layer's visibility. Clicking the top button allows you to drag the layer up and down to change the layer order. The bottom button brings up a second marking menu that allows you to change the layer's blending mode to screen, multiply, and additive and create new text layers.

Navigation and Manipulation

Navigating the canvas of SketchBook is very simple; just press the space bar. The space bar activates the Zoom/Rotate/Move Canvas tool. You can also access this tool on the toolbar and the lagoon by clicking on the magnifying glass icon. Clicking and dragging in the center zooms in and out of the canvas while clicking and dragging on the outside ring pans across the canvas.

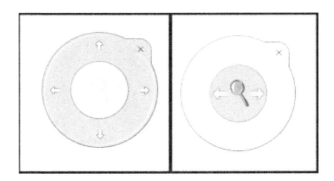

But wait. It's called the Zoom/*Rotate*/Move Canvas tool, right? Where is the option to rotate? By default the option to rotate the canvas is disabled. This is because the rotate canvas option often dramatically slows down the performance of SketchBook Pro. If your computer is extremely fast, you can enable this part of the tool under the Edit>Preferences option in the menu. You must then restart SketchBook for the change to take effect. If the performance is too slow, you can always disable it again.

Sometimes you want to manipulate the sketches and drawings you create. Although SketchBook does not offer a huge tool set for manipulating the marks you create, you can do some basic adjusting such as moving, rotating, and scaling selected areas and complete layers.

To manipulate the whole layer simply click the move/scale/rotate tool from the toolbar. It is the icon that looks like cross-hairs with outward pointing arrows, as pictured below.

The tool that opens will allow you to move, rotate, or scale the entire selected layer by simply clicking and dragging on the specified ring.

However, sometimes you only need to manipulate part of the image. In the example below, the character's left eye was drawn too low. To edit it first select the region you wish to manipulate using either the select or lasso select tool.

Select the eye that needs to be moved, then select the outermost ring from the move/rotate/scale tool to move it. When you are done, press escape.

These tools do not allow for complex manipulation, but keep in mind, this program is for drawing and sketching, not photo manipulation. This tool can be used to quickly re-proportion an arm or change the angle of a tree branch, but in the end you will have to do the detailed manipulation the old fashioned way, with a brush and an eraser.

Making Marks

Making marks inside of SketchBook is easy. Simply choose a brush and click on the canvas while moving your input device.

If you are using a device with a stylus such as a tablet or monitor then the mark will appear as the tip of your pen touches the surface. Your pressure changes specific aspects of the mark you are making, such as thickness or transparency.

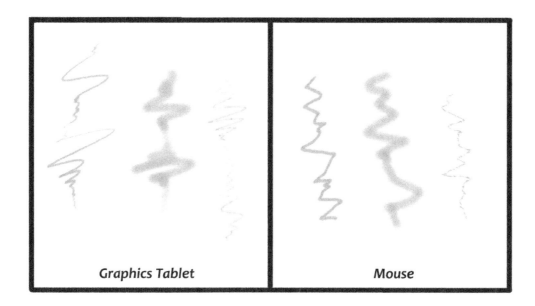

Graphics Tablet   **Mouse**

If you are using a mouse, you will not be able to change pressure; the mouse button is either clicked or it isn't. But SketchBook does a good job at faking this anyway. You will notice that if you chose the pencil brush and use your mouse to make a mark, the line will be tapered at the starting point. This is not quite the same thing as actively being able to control the line weight, but if you are using a mouse in SketchBook then it goes a long way toward making your marks look more realistic.

As mentioned earlier, you have several ways to make marks in SketchBook. By default the program will be set to allow you to draw freely. But sometimes drawing freehand is not the most ideal and efficient way to do what you need to do. Take a few minutes to explore the different options by choosing each of the below icons and learn how they work. For example, the polyline tool may be the quickest way to block out the shape of a background building. Using the line tool to find the vanishing points in two and three point perspective drawings is also very useful.

The rulers and symmetry options to the immediate left of the line options also offer some time saving techniques. Nature and design have a tendency toward symmetrical shapes. For evidence of this, just look in the mirror, at a wall plug, or at the front of your car. Symmetry is everywhere, and having these tools will help you block out symmetrical shapes and shapes with precise curves.

As a quick example of how symmetry and the rulers might help you, let's do a quick sketch of a vase. Select the pencil and turn on Symmetry Y. This will give you a vertical line down the center of your canvas. Now on one side of that line draw the profile shape of the vase.

Now turn off symmetry and turn on the Ellipse ruler. Use the square in the center to move the ruler and the circles at the left and right to resize the ruler to the correct perspective. Anything you draw with the ruler on will align to the dotted line of the ruler. Use your pencil to draw the ellipse shape that makes up the top of the vase. If you are using a tablet or pressure sensitive screen, you will notice that pressure sensitivity still affects the line you are drawing. Use this to your advantage to vary your line weight as you see fit.

Resize the ellipse ruler and move it to the bottom. Draw the front most edge of the bottom of the vase. Now what you have is a symmetrical outline sketch of the vase. You can now turn off all rulers and continue working on the drawing adding in asymmetrical shadow, color, and detail.

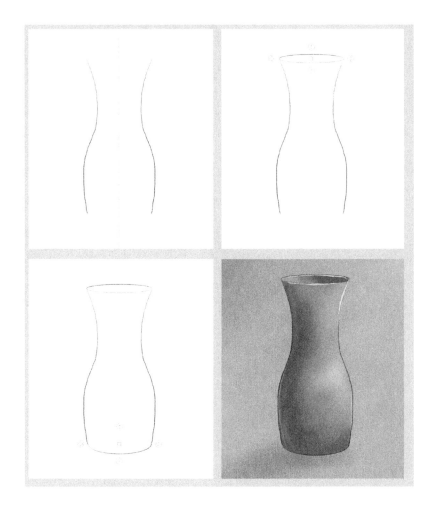

The tools offered in the PC and Mac versions of Autodesk SketchBook are simple but capable of a lot despite, if not because of their simplicity. SketchBook is designed to give you a clean and efficient way to use a digital version of the same tools artists have wielded for centuries. It is an efficient tool that gets out of your way and just lets you create.

But for as simple of a program as SketchBook is, the people at Autodesk managed to simplify it even further when bringing it to tablet and mobile devices. Most, if not all of the tools stayed intact for this transition, they are just wearing different clothes. The following two sections will explain how the same tools that we have discussed in the PC and Mac versions of SketchBook made the leap to the tablet and mobile devices.

SketchBook Pro for iPad and Android

Believe it or not, SketchBook Pro for iPad and Android is nearly as powerful as its full featured version. With many Android and iPad apps the biggest hurdle is getting over the actual device itself.

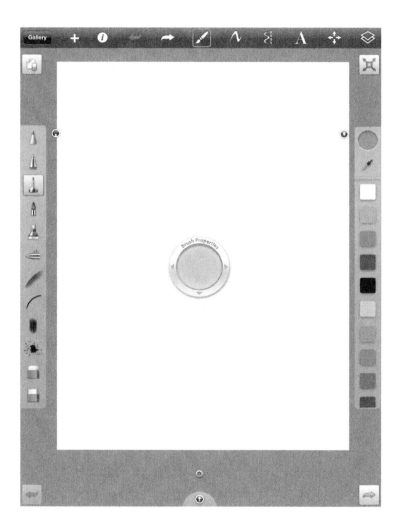

Because the primary input for tablets is either a finger or a stylus, the UI has been drastically redesigned. The thin bars along the top, right, and left sides hold all your tools. The bar along the left side is the brushes while the bar on the right is the color palette. The side bars auto-hide while you are sketching. To get them back you simply press three fingers to the screen at the same time, or tap the tiny circle at the bottom center of the screen. You can also pin the brush and color bar by tapping the thumb-tack icon beside them. This will keep them visible while you sketch.

The top bar is the toolbar. It serves as a toolbar, lagoon, and menu all in one. From this area you can access your brush preferences, symmetry, layers menu, text tool, move/rotate/scale tool, undo, redo, and all the saving and exporting options.

The brush preferences menu works similarly to the brush preferences in the PC and Mac version of SketchBook Pro, except with a slightly altered design. From this menu, you can also open the color wheel to mix and choose colors.

The layers in SketchBook Pro for iPad and Android offer all the same flexibility as the PC and Mac version, with only a slightly less intuitive interface. Rather than marking menus you have a series of icons along the bottom that serve the same functions. It isn't quite as quick and gestural of a user interface experience, but it still does the same job effectively.

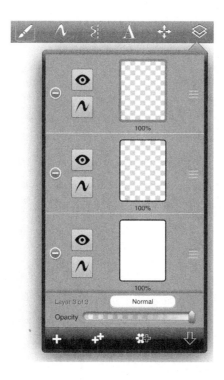

You will notice, in each of the four corners of the screen, is a single icon. While sketching, these icons auto hide. Double tapping the corners where the icons were will still perform the task of that specified icon. By default these icons are clear layer, frame canvas, undo, and redo. They can be changed and customized for whatever SketchBook action you find yourself repeating often.

The PC and Mac version of SketchBook Pro tried to severely limit the amount of shortcut keys and keyboard inputs needed to operate the program. But with no dedicated keyboard at all, the tablet version of SketchBook does not have the luxury of any shortcut keys at all. Instead SketchBook Pro for iPad and Android implements the multi touch display and the capacitive screen to take the place of these options. This combined with an altered UI provides some quick and relatively elegant solutions to the most commonly used shortcut keys.

Navigation of the canvas no longer requires you to hold down the space bar. Now you simply use the pinch zoom features that you would in navigating other tablet apps. Moving both fingers together in any given direction (as opposed to in opposite directions with the pinch) will allow you to pan around the image. By incorporating both zooming and panning into one gesture, it actually improves how quickly you can navigate the canvas. Also, tapping and holding on a single point activates a color picker to sample colors from your canvas, alleviating the need for the ALT shortcut key.

SketchBook Pro for iPad and Android replicates and interprets nearly everything that is great about the PC and Mac version of the program. However, pressure sensitivity is something that many digital artists have grown to love when using a graphics tablet or pressure sensitive display. It allows for subtle variation in line weight and opacity, but due to the limitations of the device itself, tablets do not have the option for pressure sensitive input. This is a deal breaker for many people. It is not something that is easy to overlook once you have gotten used to the additional control pressure affords you.

However, SketchBook addresses the issue simply. The lines and marks you create are simply assumed to have less pressure at the beginning and ending of the mark, and more pressure in the middle of the line. In addition, the speed at which the line is drawn affects the implied pressure sensitivity. Faster lines have a longer, more gradual thinning on the ends. This slight taper at the edges of the lines give the impression of pressure sensitivity. It is a limitation that you can either see as a hindrance or a challenge. But once you accept it you will find that you are still capable of making some very nice sketches and illustrations even without pressure sensitivity.

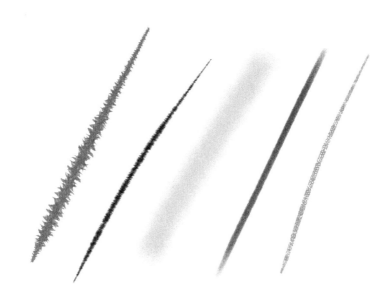

The air brush is another area where pressure sensitivity seems important. The best way to address this is to set the opacity of the airbrush to a relatively low number and build up the color with multiple strokes.

The brush resizer in the PC and Mac version of SketchBook Pro is simple. You click and drag to make the brush larger or smaller. In the tablet version of SketchBook Pro, opacity is also controlled in this same method. Dragging from side to side changes the size, while dragging up and down changes the opacity. It is a minor improvement over the PC and Mac version that goes a long way toward making the lack of pressure sensitivity more acceptable.

SketchBook Express

SketchBook Express is the free tablet version of SketchBook. Think of it as bait for SketchBook Pro for iPad and Android. It has all the same capabilities with some of the bells and whistles disabled. The UI design is the same without the convenient brush and color bars on each side of the canvas. Also you will notice that the undo button in the corner is disabled. This is one of the more helpful buttons when doing a drawing, and alone makes the $4.99 upgrade worth it.

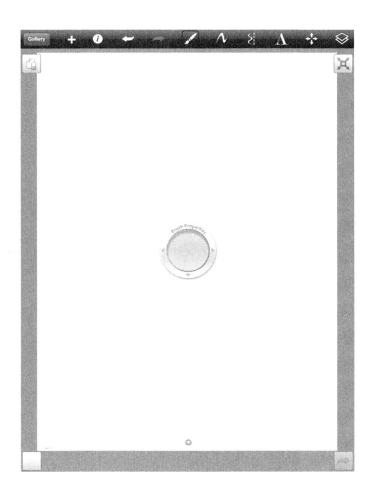

In addition several other options have been disabled on the free, express version. Maximum canvas size is capped at 1,024 x 768, while the Pro version can go as high as 2,048 x 1,536. Express only allows you to save a flattened image of your drawing, but Pro gives you the added option of exporting to a PSD file containing all your layers. Express limits your creation of custom brushes, and also restricts you to only three layers. Even though the Pro version allows you to create up to six layers, artists who use a lot of layering techniques will find even staying within that limit a challenge.

In short, SketchBook Express is a simplified version of the program that takes out many of the convenience features in an effort to spur you into purchasing the pro version. You can create good work in the express version, but unlocking the entire feature set is well worth five bucks.

Mobile Apps

SketchBook Mobile

Although phone screens are getting bigger almost every day, a phone still seems a bit small to draw your masterpiece. But if you are sitting on a park bench and the bug to draw bites you, it is nice to have it handy. Using a capacitive stylus helps matters greatly, reducing the width of your fat finger to something that is easier to control.

Being a smaller device, the UI for SketchBook Mobile is more compact than that of SketchBook Pro for iPad and Android. But surprisingly, almost all the same tool sets are packed into the 99 cent app.

The toolbar is more compact than the tablet counterpart and the brush and color bars are not taking up valuable real-estate on the tiny screen. These tools are now located in a marking menu style interface that pops up when you tap the tiny circle at the bottom center of the screen. This also brings up the toolbar, which auto-hides so you have more drawing area. The corner shortcuts persist in this version as well.

SketchBook Mobile Express

As you may have guessed, the express version of SketchBook Mobile is just a simplified version of SketchBook Mobile. The resolution is lower than the mobile version and does not have the text tool or the ability to export to a layered PSD. You also lose the ability to rotate, scale, and move layers in the express version. If you find the lack of these options annoying you really have no one to blame but yourself. The full featured version is cheaper than a small fry from the dollar menu. Just buy it already.

But if for some reason you don't have a dollar, then the mobile express version will get you by until you can find the change in your couch cushions. It is still completely capable of making fully realized sketches, and more than a little fun to play with when you are in the dentist waiting room (no doubt from eating too many cheap fries).

Example Time!

Yeah, yeah, yeah. Interface, stylus, marking menu, blah, blah, blah. Let's see this puppy in action!

Many artists have made SketchBook their primary workhorse. Browsing Autodesk's galleries you will come across amazingly skilled and talented individuals who have bent SketchBook in ways that boggle the mind. The artists at CreatureBox.com create much of the drawing and inking in SketchBook.

Paris Christou is the creator of the popular pin-up character Cherry. He offers classes in how to draw Cherry, and you guessed it, he works in SketchBook.

More of Paris' work can be found at www.ToonBoxStudio.com, as well as his popular instructional pin-up drawing series. Watching over the shoulder of an artist who uses the program daily is a great way to become familiar with the tips and tricks that might not seem so obvious.

The following sections contain guides to several different work flows and tool usages in the different versions of SketchBook. The illustrations were all created by the author of this book, who is a professional animator, not a professional illustrator. Whether you doodle, create animation thumbnails, or paint masterpieces, SketchBook can serve as a useful tool in your daily work flow. This section is for you to explore how you might like to use it yourself.

SketchBook Pro - Scared Ted's Head

The first example sketch we will look at is a quick ten minute doodle completed in the PC version of SketchBook Pro using a Wacom Intuos tablet. It was not intended to be a finished illustration, simply a quick character concept sketch to get some ideas.

First, start with the symmetry Y tool to split the image vertically down the center. Using the pencil brush, sketch a quick outline of the character's facial shapes. The symmetry tool allows for rapid form building of the head. Using sweeping long strokes, find the overall shapes of the character's head, nose, lips, mustache, neck, brows, eyes, and hair. Don't worry about putting too much detail in the sketch, it is more of a form and shape finding exploration. In this example, the character has a boxy head and wide round eyes and nose. Because of his surprised look, let's call him scared Ted.

After you are happy with the shapes you have created for Ted's head, create a new layer and place it under the sketchy line layer. Using the marker brush, color in the skin areas of Ted's head and shoulders. Placing this new layer under the lines layer will allow for the color to show through in the empty space without covering up the original line work.

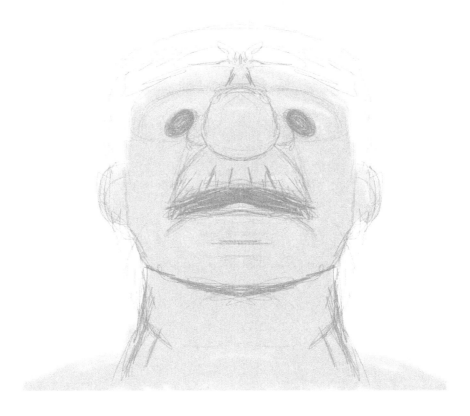

Next, create another layer on top of the base skin color layer. Then, using the marker, put an additional color base to Ted's shirt, mustache, hair, and brows. Also use this layer to fill Ted's eyes in with white, however use the paint brush to do this rather than the marker. The marker is an additive brush meaning you cannot add a lighter color to the top of a darker color. They work like real markers, and white markers don't really exist. But white paint does.

It is also interesting to note that up to this point all the color has also been applied using the symmetry tool. But at this time, you can turn it off to start getting a little asymmetry.

Next, create another new layer on top of the previous color layers, but still under the original line sketch. Using the airbrush tool, add a bit of asymmetrical shadows to imply a light source coming from the upper left side of the image. Considering your light source and sticking to it are crucial to developing believable forms.

To break up the even skin colors you can also add some pink blush to his cheeks and nose.

Still using the airbrush, add some highlights to the upper edges of some of the shapes on his face to give a little more credibility to the light source and to imply highlights on his skin. This will also help to round out his nose a bit.

Because this is just a quick sketch it is not necessary to extensively outline the shapes, but some of the forms are still feeling a bit vague. Using a small version of the airbrush, add in some more clearly defined edged around his chin and eyes. This is also a good time to fill in his mouth shape. The asymmetrical mouth opening was improvised at this step. Feel free to play with other mouth shapes and how they affect Ted's expression.

It is also important to note that this is the first layer on top of the line layer. You will see that the black covers up some of the previous line work around the mouth and neck line.

Finally, to pull the image together, use a marker and a dark, grayish brown to add an implied background. The turbulent lines also add to the surprise on Ted's face. What on earth could have scared him so? Perhaps he is looking at the price of a new Cintiq.

SketchBook Pro - Strawberry

Next let's create a slightly more refined illustration. As with any project you should always start with an idea, and from that idea gather as much reference images as possible.

A quick internet search will provide you with an abundance of reference images. Rather than directly copying any specific photo, spend ten minutes or so combing through these images and analyzing the consistent visual elements that make up a strawberry. Use this information to form a solid idea of what you want your image to look like. This planning stage can take many forms depending on your own work flow and the complexity of the illustration. Since this is just a single strawberry, your planning consists primarily of deciding the strawberry's placement and angle.

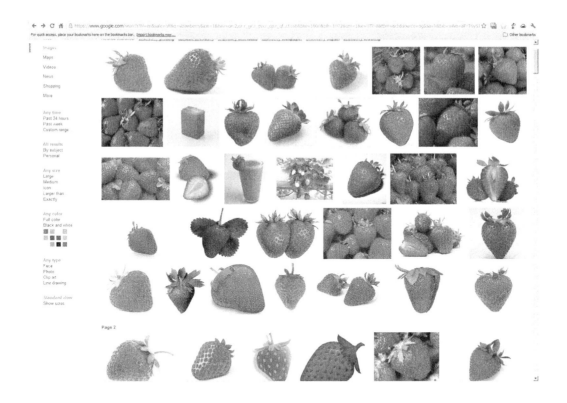

After gathering references it is time to open SketchBook Pro. The first thing you should do is raise the image resolution by going to Image>Image size. The example was created using a resolution of 300 pixels per inch. When making decisions about resolution, consider the final output of the illustration. You can always lower the resolution, but it is much harder to raise the resolution of an image without experiencing pixilation.

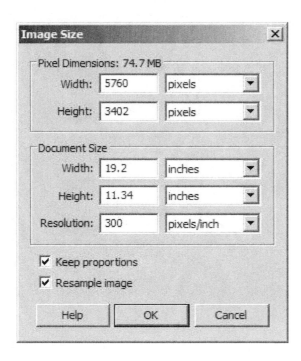

Chose a base color by using the eye dropper on one of the reference photos. In fact if you take a few minutes to build an entire palette of colors by sampling images, it will save you time later.

To create the base shape of the strawberry create a large, red splotch in the general area you want it to be.

From looking at the reference images, you can tell that this is an illustration that will require you to use the airbrush quite a bit. So to save time later, let's define the shape of this strawberry in a bit of a non-traditional way. Create a layer above the red splotch layer, and with a hard gray paint brush, paint the inverse of the shape you want the berry to be. This will leave a perfect, strawberry shaped area of transparency in the gray layer that will allow the red of the layer underneath to show through in the shape of a strawberry.

You can see this more clearly in the illustration below where the gray layer's transparency has been turned down to about 50 percent.

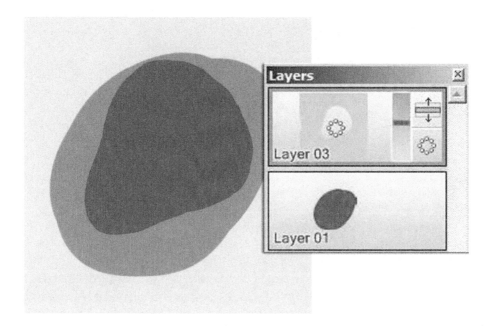

This may seem like more work than it is worth at first. After all, it is a lot easier to simply paint in and erase away areas to sculpt the red shape. But the benefits of using this method is that it allows you to paint without worrying about going outside of the lines.

The next step in the process will illustrate this point. Create a new layer above the red base but below the gray framing top layer. Using a large soft airbrush and a darker shade of the same red, add a soft shadow along the bottom and side of the strawberry to indicate a light source from above as well as the imperfect shape. The below illustration shows the new shadows with and without the top gray layer framing the shape.

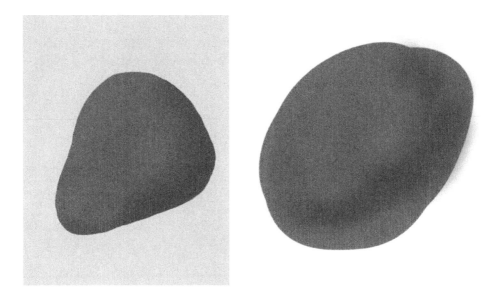

Continuing with the top gray layer visible, airbrush an additional darker shadow along the bottom edge to further ground the strawberry.

Then, using a large airbrush and a very light pink color, add an overall highlight layer to the shape of the strawberry. Again, make the highlight a bit inconsistent to indicate the dips and dents in the strawberry's form. With a hard eraser, carve a systematic series of concentric holes in this highlight layer. These holes will indicate the indentions where the seeds will be.

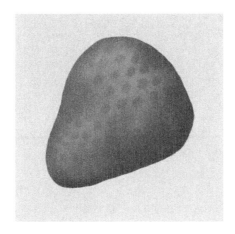

Next, using a smaller airbrush and a nearly white color, add brighter highlights along the bottom edge of each seed indention to indicate highlights from the above light source. Also, inside each of the seed indentions, make a small dark red shadow to indicate the shadow cast by the seed.

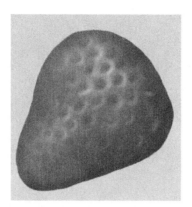

On another layer, using a small hard paintbrush and a yellow color sampled from a reference image, put tiny dots inside each of the seed indentions. Then using a darker shade of the same yellow, paint shadows along the bottom of each seed.

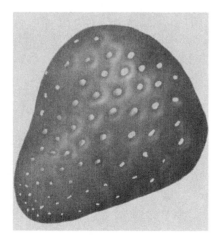

Moving on to the leaves of the strawberry, create a new layer, but this time create the layer on top of the gray framing layer. Paint a green shape using a hard paintbrush and a color sampled from a reference image. Refine the shape with a hard eraser.

On a new layer, using darker and lighter shades of green sampled from reference and a soft airbrush, paint the details of the leaf. On areas where your go outside of the green region, erase any unwanted marks with a hard eraser.

At this point the strawberry itself is looking pretty good but it needs to be tied in to the environment better. Again, create a new layer on top of the gray framing layer. Using a dark gray, paint shadows on the floor as well as additional shadows along the bottom of the strawberry. Set this layer to the multiply blend mode. Then add darker shadows where needed using darker shades of gray or even black. Adjust the opacity of this layer to achieve the shadow intensity you want. To remove and sculpt the shadows, use a soft eraser brush.

Finally, create a new top layer and set that layer to a screen blend mode. Add highlights and rim lights along the top and bounce light along the bottom. Adjust the opacity accordingly to get the final result.

SketchBook Tablet - Troll

The tablet version of SketchBook Pro takes a bit of time to get used to if you are coming directly from the PC and Mac version. The difference between the capacitive touch screen on a tablet and the active digitizer of a Wacom tablet or pressure sensitive screen is that you cannot predict perfectly where the lines you are drawing will start and stop. With a Wacom tablet you can hover the pen slightly off the surface to position the cursor before pressing the pen to make a mark. Android devices and iPads don't offer this luxury. In addition, the input device on an iPad or Android, generally your finger or a capacitive stylus, has a larger margin of error because of its width. This will take some adjustment. The best course of action is to experiment and do a few throw-away sketches before starting anything you plan on hanging on the refrigerator.

 Because of this input difficulty, the tablet version of SketchBook Pro lends itself more to painterly, gestural sketches and illustrations that require less precision. But that does not mean cleaner crisp illustrations are impossible. So for this illustration, let's do an inked, cartoon style character, despite the difficulty of precision.

First choose a background color, although this can always be changed later. Using the paint bucket tool from the brushes menu, fill the background with the color.

Then, on a new layer using the pencil tool and a mid range gray, do a sketch to get the overall shapes of the character, in this case, a troll. You will notice that he is primarily constructed out of simple shapes and forms. Some people prefer to do a second sketch pass on top of this to refine the details.

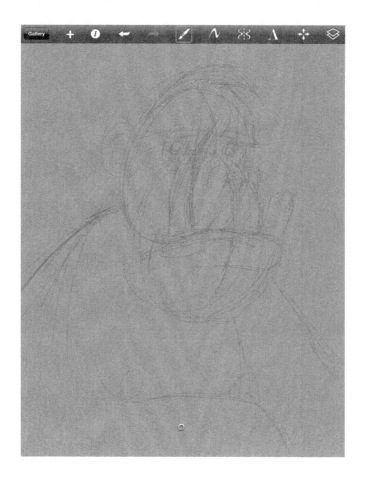

Next. create a new layer, and using the color black and the pencil, create crisper, bolder inking lines. This step is where the undo button comes in handy. Make your marks quick and gestural to get a smooth clean line. If the line is incorrect, double tap the lower left corner to undo the stroke. Repeat this process over and over until you get the line you want. This is a good technique when inking in any package, but it is particularly helpful in the tablet version of SketchBook Pro.

After all the inking lines are complete, use the eraser to refine the shapes and overlaps of the lines.

Next, under the line layer, create a new layer. Using a hard solid paint brush, paint the base colors for the troll. Don't worry too much about staying within the lines. After all the color is in place, use a hard eraser to remove any marks outside the lines.

It is also a good idea to paint small swatches of the colors you use on this later in an unused corner of the image. You can erase them later, but it will allow you to quickly resample the colors to create variations of color or repair future mistakes.

Next, to soften hard lines where two colors meet, use the airbrush. First sample one color by pressing and holding your finger or stylus to a color you wish to sample. Air brush over the sharp line with this color. Then resample the color softer blended color to get an in-between color. Resample and airbrush the area till you have a smooth transition from one color to another.

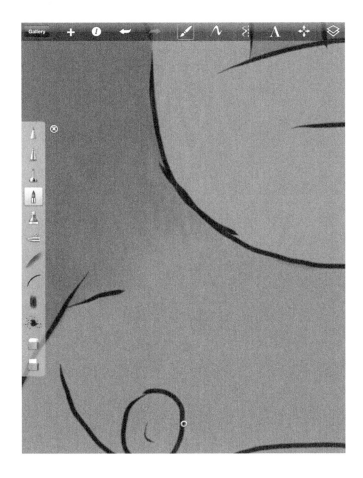

Next, on a new layer, use a dark brown color and a hard paintbrush to paint in the shadow areas and crevices that would occlude light. Again, don't worry too much about going outside of the lines.

Set this new shadow layer to the multiply blending mode.

Use a hard eraser to sculpt the shadow and erase areas that went outside of the lines.

You can repeat the entire shadow step to create a highlight on the troll, except use a lighter color and set the layer to screen blending mode instead of multiply.

For the next step we will add hair and texture to the troll's body. Select a textured brush that you like, testing it on a new layer. Feel free to replicate the settings pictured below.

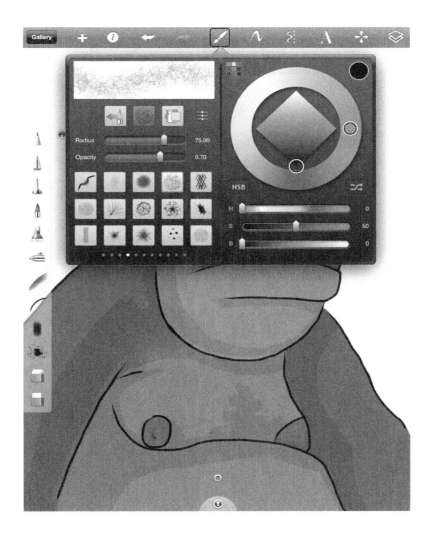

Once you have a textured brush you like, lightly add in darker layers of hair to his back, shoulders, and arms.

Paint in additional texture to the background to frame the image.

Finally, to tie the image together, create a new layer on top of all the others. This will be what is called a glaze layer. Fill the layer with a single color, preferably within a hue already found in the illustration. In this case, blue works nicely. Set the glaze layer to the multiply blend mode and adjust the opacity very low, to something like five percent.

The glaze layer adds a level of cohesiveness to all the colors in the final image.

SketchBook Mobile - Box

Creating an illustration in SketchBook Mobile is a very similar work flow to that of the tablet version. The difference is that you are working on a screen that is approximately the size of a business card. For precision, it is highly suggested that you invest a few dollars in a capacitive pen for detailed work.

But despite the small stature of the device, you can accomplish some very nice detailed and even technical renders with some handy work flow techniques. For this example, you will create two point perspective drawing of a box.

First change your mark style from free to line. This will allow you to draw perfectly straight lines. Create your horizon line with a pencil or small paintbrush. Also indicate, with an x or a mark, your two desired vanishing points.

Next, draw a perfectly vertical line to indicate front most edge of the box. Then draw connecting lines to the vanishing points for the top and bottom edges of the box. To complete the box shape, draw the back two vertical edges of the box. Don't worry about crossing over lines or keeping these lines clean, they are simply guide lines for the rest of the drawing.

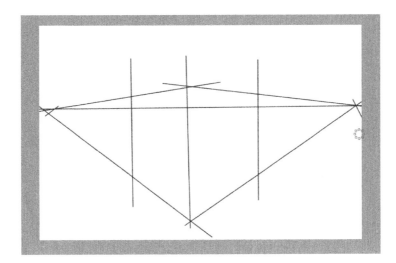

Now lower the transparency on the guide lines layer and create a new layer beneath it.

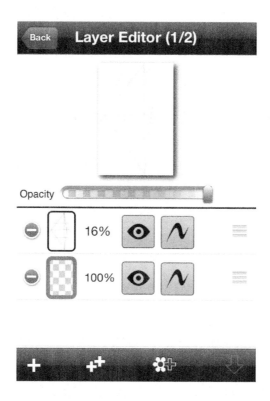

Using a medium paintbrush, color one side of the box. Don't worry about staying within the lines. You will fix that in the next step.

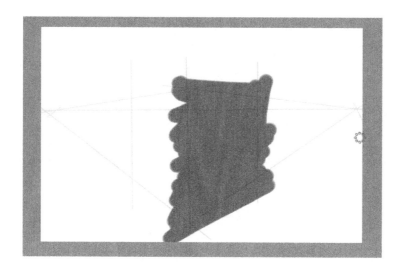

This step is one you will find very useful when using the mobile or tablet versions of SketchBook. Because of the nature of the capacitive touch screen, it is hard to predict precisely where a line you are creating will actually start. Even the more precise pens have a margin of error that is not really acceptable when trying to do detail work. The solution is to add color to the canvas and then remove the color strategically to get detail. So rather than stay in the lines, you will paint more than is needed and erase away the rest.

The technique is simple. If you erase in an area where there is no paint then nothing changes. So start erasing outside of the area you wish to erase, making rapid side to side marks with your finger or stylus. Slowly move inward erasing bits as you get closer.

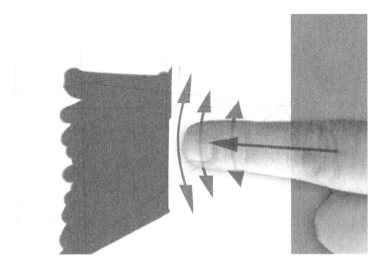

Do this for all four sides of the box till you have a single side cleanly colored in.

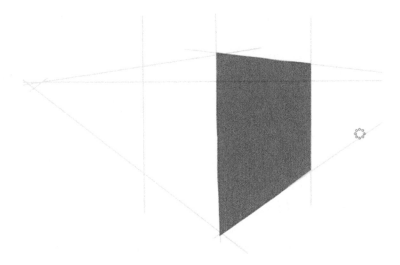

Repeat this process to create the second side of the box on a new layer using a lighter shade of blue.

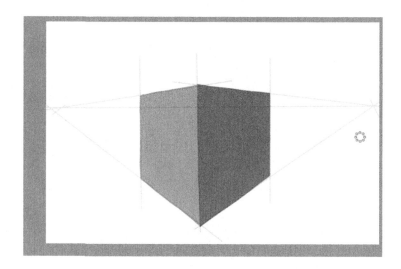

At this point you can hide the guide layer if you wish. Now you have a very simple, flat shaded box. The technique of painting outside the desired area and then erasing away the unwanted bits can be used to create soft shading as well. On a new layer, choose a darker blue and use the airbrush to add dark areas to the inside corner of the box. Again, don't worry about going outside of the desired area.

Using a hard brush, erase the areas of color you don't want. This will give you a hard line with a softer falloff.

Repeat the process on the other side of the box, adjusting for color. You can also add highlighted areas this way as well.

Finally add some shadows to root the box to the ground. Starting with a light blue color will help give the perception of bounce light. This is also a good time to add a highlight down the closest edge to make it feel slightly rounded.

Add darker shadows to finalize the image.

SketchBook Pro: J Haines Dirksmein's CDV

Anyone who has ever taken a drawing class in school can relate to this story. You go to the art store to buy your supplies. You get pencils, charcoal, and maybe some pastels. You get a few sketchbooks and a large pad of drawing paper, and then in a whim of reckless abandon, you decide to splurge on a few sheets of nice colored or textured drawing paper, something fancy.

You take the fancy paper to class with you every day, but nothing ever seems to be the perfect drawing to warrant breaking out the $2.50 sheet of paper. After all, you are in college, that is like seven packs of Ramen noodles. So you hold on to it for months. You even put it in a special place in your dorm so your stupid friends don't use it as a beer coaster.

Finally the day comes. The perfect drawing presents itself. You break out the fancy paper, you grab your best box of pastels, and you let the muse dance in your soul as you start drawing. And then two minutes in, oops, you ruined the drawing.

It is scenarios like this that make experimentation with new ideas and media difficult. Oh yeah, everyone wants to try to paint with an airbrush, but no one wants to spend eighty dollars to buy one just to see if they like it. That is what makes programs like SketchBook, and the digital art revolution as a whole so beneficial to new artists. Want to try painting on a pink textured canvas? All it will cost you is the time it takes to click the paint bucket tool. This ease of experimentation unshackles the artist and lets them explore ideas that would have been too costly otherwise.

So for this exercise let's try doing a drawing on a colored canvas. You will primarily be using the pencil brush and one layer, just like you would in a real pencil drawing. In the case of this drawing, our subject is an old carte de visite (CDV - a calling card popular in the late 1800's and early 1900's). It has a signature at the bottom that appears to read J Haines Dirksmein, so that's what we will call him. It is also important to note that since most carte de visites were popular in the late 1800's, most of them are now in the public domain and completely free to use as reference or subject matter.

First prepare the canvas in the format you prefer. In this case, change the orientation of the canvas to a portrait dimension and fill the bottom most layer with a light to mid-tone gray. When picking the shade of gray, consider the mood of the piece. You want the gray to represent the most common shade in the image, so every darker shade you add will represent shadow and every lighter will represent highlight. If you want your image to seem moodier and darker, then you might select a darker gray, and vice versa if you want a lighter, daylight feeling.

Just in case you want to later change your background choice, create a new layer for the line work. This is the layer which you will be doing most of your drawing. Some people work in more than one layer, and that is fine, but don't be afraid to fall back on your traditional chops and go forth fearlessly on one layer. You will find that mistakes are still easier to fix than on paper.

The remainder of the instruction for this lesson could easily read, "Just draw like you normally would." But we will walk through the steps used to create this drawing anyway. Create a quick proportion sketch to get the general shapes of the head neck and shoulders in the drawing.

Next start filling in and defining features of the head and face. Feel free to stay loose and sketchy with your lines and just erase unneeded marks later. The beauty of this application is that it allows you all the freedom to work the way you are comfortable with without the fear of making a permanent mistake. If you make a mark you don't like use CTRL+Z or the undo button to undo it.

Work your way toward more fine details. Zoom in to areas and adjust your brush size to get the fidelity you want from each mark.

The lasso tool will allow you to select areas that were incorrectly drawn and move, scale, and rotate them into the ideal position. This is a nice way to quickly re-proportion areas that were sketched incorrectly rather than redrawing them.

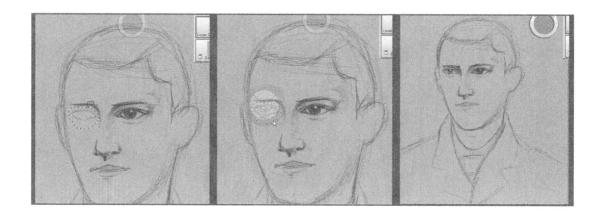

Continue adding in more details and shading. You can vary your line color as well to make subtle shading less dependent on the pressure of your pen. This is particularly helpful in areas with very faint shading like the cheek.

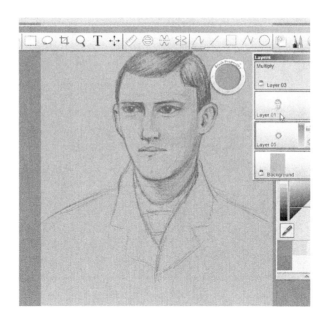

We started with a light gray background to give us an even neutral shade. But J Haines' jacket is darker and his shirt is nearly white. So rather than sketch in all the subtle shade variation, you can simply fill in the background color with a separate base shade for those particular areas. If you like the textured effect of the pencil, you can also do this shading with a textured brush.

Continue to add more shadows to the darker areas. Then with a white pencil add in the highlight areas. This can be done at any stage in the process. Ideally you will be able to use these techniques to develop a tonal range that goes from sharp highlights to dark shadows.

SketchBook Pro: Tractor

SketchBook Pro can be used to replicate many different styles and medias. So it should be no surprise that you can use it as a complete digital painting suite if you wish. For this example, we will paint an old tractor in a field based off this reference image.

Painting in SketchBook relies heavily on sampling different colors and using the right brush for the job. So after creating your canvas to the shape and resolution you desire, import the reference image into the file and resize it to fit into the top corner of your screen. Hint: this may require you opening this eBook on a PC and capturing the image with the print screen option. It is also a good idea to keep the reference image on its own dedicated layer so you can hide and unhide it.

Now you have the reference image in the file you can quickly sample colors from the original image using the eye dropper tool (ALT key). You can also print the image or keep it open on a second monitor to refer to while you paint.

Next let's select a brush to start off this painting. This choice will depend on the style you prefer. In this example, start with an existing brush from preset 1. It has a decent amount of texture and is really good for blocking in the early colors of the painting.

Using light additive strokes, color in the background with a darker color from the grassy background. You can also add some lighter hues on top of that to give a rough backdrop that represents the tonal variation of the grassy field.

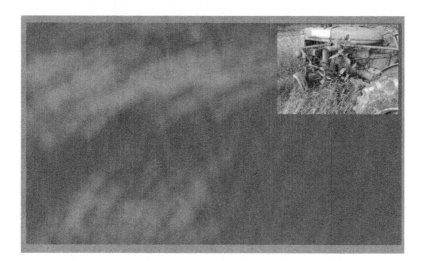

Create another layer and quickly block in the shapes and forms of the tractor using colors sampled from the original source image.

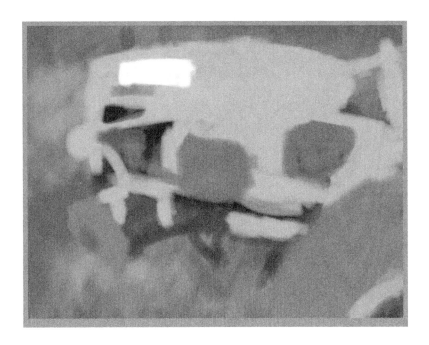

Painting in any digital program, and some might even say with real paint, is a series of refinement passes. Work from larger more generalized shapes toward detailed refined areas.

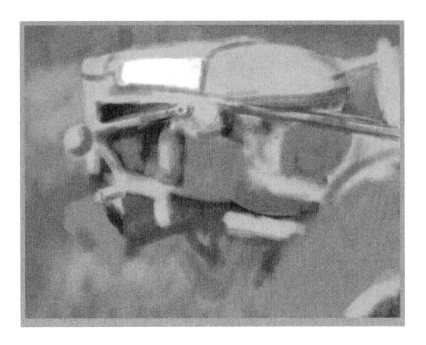

For the most part, the remainder of the painting process for this project is to sample from the reference image or from the painting itself, and use those colors to add more details and enhancements to the areas that are vague or not clearly defined.

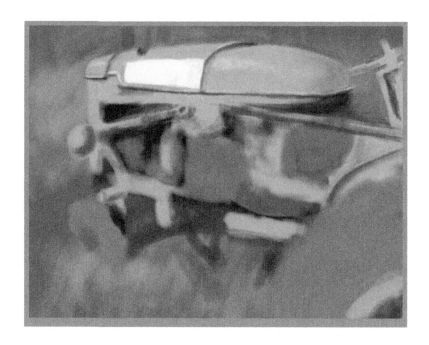

It is also good to consider which brush is best fitting for the task you are trying to achieve. If you need a smooth falloff of color then the airbrush is a good tool. Harder edged solid colors made by the paint brush are best for the areas that need to be filled in completely. Pencils add sharp, crisp, thin lines. And if you want a small, thin, softer line, try a very small airbrush.

Sometimes brushes can be used to solve specific texture related painting challenges. In the case of the tractor's rust, it could be manually created using a lot of tedious small marks with a pencil, or you could use the dotted_2 brush, with just a few alterations, to get a very quick and pleasing rust effect.

Adding foreground elements at a relatively early stage will eliminate the need to paint details that may be covered later. So at this point, adding a bit more information to the grass and plants is a good place to direct your focus.

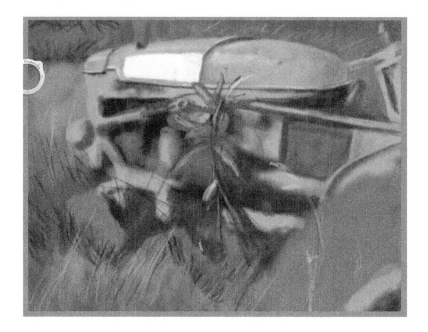

Detailing intricate and complicated areas, like the engine and mechanical parts of the tractor, can be time consuming, but it is those niceties that add a level or believability to the piece.

Deciding when a painting is "finished" is partially dictated by the artist's particular style, but it is always important to maintain a level of cohesiveness in the final image. You can create a glaze layer, similar to the ogre piece created earlier. You can also frame the image to guide the eye inward using a dark overlay around the edges of the image (or light depending on the image's mood).

Conclusion

When working with any 2D art software it is easy to become entranced with all the bells and whistles and fancy high-end features, but some artists just want a clean, easy to use, and responsive tool that works similarly to the real world tools to which they are accustomed. That is where SketchBook shines. And surprisingly it has also managed to make a very astute leap to the tablet and mobile devices without losing many of its crucial features.

SketchBook is not for everyone or every project. It does one thing very well; it allows you to get ideas out of your head and into a computer as painlessly as possible. It takes the skills you have learned as an artist and gives you a digital vehicle with which to use them. And if that is what you are needing, that is what Autodesk SketchBook is offering.

Printed by Amazon Italia Logistica S.r.l.
Torrazza Piemonte (TO), Italy

13639662R00055